Miss Lillie's Home Training

Life Lessons for Your Soul

M Kirby Toombs

ISBN: 978-1-6847-1559-6 (sc)
ISBN: 978-1-6847-1560-2 (e)

Lulu Publishing Services rev. date: 01/08/2020

Dedication

Quoting Miss Lillie, my Mama, "Resolve to see, Resolve to be. Resolve to hear, Resolve to feel. But most of all, resolve to get up, move on and live happily and completely."

Dedicated to each one of you who resolved to walk with me on this journey, sometimes pushing me, sometimes pulling me, but always supporting me.

Vicky Phelps
Jane Elrod, Sally Davis, and Tommie Jones
Barbara and Nancy Westbrook
Ledia Galbraith and Samaritan Potter
Ray Woods
Brenda Pinkston
Emmett and Faye Toombs
Baby Dog

Contents

Preface

As I sat down to write a Preface for <u>Miss Lillie's Home Training</u>, I tried to imagine a reader seeing the book on the shelf and wondered what would spark interest enough for someone to want to spend time with Miss Lillie and listen to her Life Lessons. I've gladly listened to her over the years, but then I would. You see, Miss Lillie is my Mama, Lillian Edna Hall Toombs. Born in the 1920's and named Lillie Edna. She actually changed her name to Lillian because she thought "Lillie" was just too Southern. I won't say exactly what year she was born; Mama was touchy about that. Indeed, I doubt my Daddy ever really knew her exact age, but that was just fine by him. My Daddy worshipped my Mama until the day he passed. He never saw a wrinkle on her face, and every time he looked at her, you could see love in his eyes, true unequivocal love. They often walked hand in hand, and Mama didn't even learn to drive until late in life, preferring instead to enter a vehicle from the driver's side, scoot over a bit and sit next to Daddy wherever they ventured.

But back to Miss Lillie, my Mama. As I said, she was born in the 1920's, in Lebanon, Tennessee, to Charlie Lemuel Hall and Alice Greene McIntyre, one of eight children, not the baby, but definitely the baby girl. Now, in the South there's well-to-do, getting by, disadvantaged, poor and dirt poor. The Halls started out married life fairly well-to-do, but quickly fell into the dirt poor category. As more and more children were born, my grandfather, an alcoholic, began drinking constantly, became abusive to his family and spent more time in jail than at home. Sadly, Mama's early years were filled with hunger, family squabbles and much abuse. Mama's tale of her father chasing her mother around and around the house with a switchblade used to chill my bones, but in true "Miss Lillie" fashion, Mama took lemons and made lemonade. She worshipped her mother and bore little ill will toward her father's disease to be honest. In fact, she credits his alcoholism to her dislike for excessive drinking, preferring instead to channel her lifestyle into books, education and family.

At the tender age of six, and as my grandfather had been in jail for several months, food was nonexistent in the house. One of Mama's older sisters even stole a rooster from a home nearby at Christmas so the family could eat, and the neighbors brought potatoes for soup adding to that meager Christmas meal. Mama saw her mother peeling the potatoes and eating the peelings so the children could all share the potatoes, but Mama wouldn't eat if her mother didn't, in spite of the peelings, so she got no Christmas meal. The next day, the county Sheriff came and took all the children, Miss Lillie included, to a school in Nashville for disadvantaged children. Mama recalled she wouldn't let her mother see her cry as they drove away, and looking out the window of that patrol car, Mama waved her little hand and resolved in her soul to make the best of the situation. She was six years old remember, and little did she know it would be six long years before she would see her dear mother again.

Why have I shared such intimate details of my Mama's past you ask? Because in spite of and maybe as a result of such trauma, Mama made a conscious choice at that young age to not only survive, but to excel. She loved her years at TPS/TIS in Nashville, the school mentioned earlier, and in fact graduated valedictorian. She was awarded a full scholarship to George Peabody College in Nashville, now a division of Vanderbilt University, but turned that down to marry my Daddy, and to raise a family. She wanted to make sure her own family had everything she didn't growing up. These memories prove she did just what she set out to do. Mama never met a stranger and never stopped learning. Always a voice for the underdog, Mama believed in people. I recognized early on my Mama was special, at times quirky and unusual, but always full of joy, imagination and humor.

When Mama passed, I put pen to paper as a means to combat grief, remembering snippets of things she said, and moments we had shared over the years. What I found as I started writing was a lifetime of wonder and insight. These fifty-two life lessons from my Mama, Miss Lillie, are representative of the person Mama was and continues to be. I hope you enjoy each one, and I'm blessed to share with you what I was taught, my home training, truly life lessons for the soul.

Life Lesson #1

Snapping Beans and Dipping Snuff

Sipping coffee in my garden this morning, listening to the bees buzzing and the birds arguing with each other, the sounds began to blend into almost a white noise, lulling me peacefully back through my brain's memories. For some reason I began to hum a little tune softly to myself. I couldn't get the tune out of my mind, and yet I couldn't quite remember where I'd heard it, but as the words took shape in my head, I traveled back to a warm Summer's day long before. A young boy, legs dangling off the porch, I was listening to my Granny and my Mama talking, both of them sitting in a two-seater swing on our farmhouse porch in Smyrna, Tennessee. They both had big old white dish tubs on their laps snapping green beans, occasionally my Granny would dip her snuff.

There was a lull in the conversation and Granny began to hum, then sing an old song from her childhood. I liked the tune so I got up and plopped myself at their feet as any Southern boy from that time might do and listened. Granny sang and Mama joined in, so it had to be a song they both somehow collectively knew. The sad words began to weave pictures in my head of a time long before me, before Mama and even before my Granny. The song was called "When this Cruel War is Over," written in the 1860's. Now my Granny was born in 1880, so she learned it at her Mama's knee.

Granny had a sweet, crisp sad lament to her voice. Tears began to run down her wrinkled face and my Mama's too. I stood up and wiped the tears from their cheeks, only to realize I was crying too, no idea why. Granny and Mama hugged me tight, picked me up and put me between them on that old swing. Granny put a handful of beans on my lap and said, "Make yourself useful little sir. Someday you'll remember that all cruel things come to an end and you'll find peace on a porch, maybe even snapping beans."

I looked up at my Mama and she smiled at me, then she winked at Granny. Both of them wiped away tears on little white embroidered handkerchiefs they tucked in their apron pockets and the only sounds then were the bees, the birds, the creaking of that old swing, and the snapping of those green beans. The love, though, surrounding me on that swing has carried me through many hardships and obviously, as today, creeps out of a tiny boy's memories even as he's become a very old man, sitting quietly in his garden, on his porch.

If you've never heard the song, "When this Cruel War is Over," research it. It'll transform you and move you. Why, it may even trigger a "snapping beans and dipping snuff" moment for you. I hope so.

Life Lesson #2

⌒·//·⌒

Clarity and a Rocking Chair

Have you ever noticed that most people as they age buy rocking chairs? No Southern porch or courtyard is ever really complete without one. Whether wooden, wicker, wrought iron or plastic, those little rockers connected to a chair's feet create a bliss that's hard to describe. Perhaps the movement harkens back to the comfort of being rocked to sleep as a child or perhaps the older brain needs a little "rock" now and then to stay in tune, a little akin to a good shaken martini, but that's another life lesson entirely.

Coffee in hand and a steady rhythmic rock in my chair, my little garden is an oasis. Watching the squirrel munching on his special treats, listening to the morning call of a dove perched on my neighbor's roof, I was lulled into a trance. My old rocker's creaking was slowly matched by a second rocker's sound and the sweet voice of my Mama said, "Take this time to find clarity in the chaos. Clear your mind of can't. What we see in others depends on the clarity of the window through which we look." With my eyes half shut, I said, "Yes ma'am." I half expected to see my Mama's little smiling face, but the rocker across from me was still and silent. I realized my Mama had spoken those words to me long before, and yet perhaps this morning she had visited again to make sure I listened. Not missing a beat, I shook my head and smiled. "Yes ma'am," I said again, "I hear you."

So take a minute today, and if you don't have a rocking chair, you may want to rethink your next furniture purchase. Some people may run and others may walk for awareness. Perhaps we just need a good "rocking" for clarity.

And now back to that shaken martini…

Life Lesson #3

Friendships and Maple Trees

In late October 2009, my Mama woke me on a bright but cold Sunday morning, ready for a road trip. This rarely happened and because of that, I could tell there was an urgency to the request. She was dressed, bejeweled and even had her hair picked out (what's "picked out" you ask – something only a Southern lady of a specific and older generation would understand I suppose. Mama's hairstyle was teased and sprayed hard into a smashable but flattering configuration that needed no styling, just a hair pick and a lifting back to life, sort of like fix-a-flat for a low-aired tire.)

As I put her wheelchair in the trunk I asked her where we were going. She handed me a tiny clipped obituary from the local paper with an address in Smithville, Tennessee. James Jessup, 91, survived by his widow, Sarah Miller Jessup. Married 70 years it went on to say. Mama retrieved the little newsprint and we were off.

Now, traveling with my Mama the distance from Smyrna, Tennessee to Smithville was challenging at best since Mama needed to make pit stops every 20 minutes or so. But we managed and at every stop she shared a bit of Mama wisdom and insight, each one a life lesson unto itself and each one I'll have to share with you at another time.

As we neared Smithville, Mama began directing, turn right here, down the road a mile, turn left through the gate and up the hill. I was astonished. I didn't know my Mama had ever been to Smithville, let alone knew it well enough to give me directions, but we arrived at a well-worn but lovingly cared for farm house on the side of a hill. Out of the door walked a tall thin lady Mama's age, same hard sprayed hairstyle and infectious smile. "Lillie Hall," she said (my Mama's maiden name is Hall) and Mama almost squealed, "Sarah Miller." They hugged for what seemed like an eternity and we were ushered into the house. These were obviously two old friends long absent.

Listening to them talking like school girls over cups of coffee strong enough to knock a mule over, I pieced together their long friendship. School together in the 30's in Nashville and separated after WWII, now back together late in life. On and on they talked of marriage, children, joys and sorrows. I dozed often and when finally the only sound I heard was the wall clock ticking, I opened my eyes to see their little hands intertwined, both silent and staring out the kitchen window, the life bond between them still strong.

When ready to go, and Mama safely tucked into the car, Mrs. Jessup leaned down and pointing up the hill behind the house, she said, "Lillie, long ago I planted two trees for us high up on that hill behind the house, she said, "as a testament to our friendship. Look up." There in amongst the green and brown sparkled two red and orange Maple trees just barely touching but bright and strong. "There they'll stand long after we're gone," she said. "Two girls laughing still in the Autumn of their lives."

Mama smiled and hugged her friend. I heard her whisper, "Sarah, I've missed you so over the years, not the I haven't seen you in a while kind of miss you, but the I wish you were here at this very moment kind of miss you. Autumn truly is a second Spring when every leaf is a flower, even life's final Autumn."

And down the driveway we went. I noticed neither lady looked back at each other but both held their hands high in farewell. Mama was quiet on the way home but looked at me once and touching my face with her tiny wrinkled hand, said, "Autumn paints in colors that Summer has never seen." Mama passed the next Spring and I read that Mrs. Jessup had passed that Winter.

Guard your long time friendships closely, letting their varied colors deepen and shine as time passes. Just like Maple trees, those friendships are truly life's final Autumn jewels.

Life Lesson #4

ु॰#ॱ

Jardin de L'esprit.
Garden of the Mind

Rarely, come to think of it if ever, do I know the origins of one of my sweet little Mama's life lessons. This morning, though, while rocking and drinking a cup of coffee, the first of many chicory-laced brews to jumpstart my old brain, I remembered a phrase my Mama used to say when life's hard knock bruises faded far too slowly. Instead of crying, "Woe is me," Mama used to sigh once, then twice and say, "Jardin de L'esprit." She'd repeat it three times and by the third iteration, her smile would return and she'd move on, dropping whatever adversity like a wool coat on a warm Spring day.

As I said, I rarely knew where my Mama's wisdom originated, but this particular teaching, I did. When I was young, a teenager in fact, I ran away from home, far away. Not trying to escape my parents or my upbringing, it couldn't have been a more loving environment, but running away to a more tolerant place than I found in Smyrna, Tennessee. In Smyrna at that time I was bullied, made fun of, called names and harassed unmercifully. To put it simply, I didn't fit the small town norm. My life choices led me down a path few in my town trod and if they did they kept it secret and behind closed doors. The latter more than likely, but for a 16 year old child who couldn't keep his true self hidden, peer pressure can be devastating. I had one of two choices, suicide or leave. I'm still here so fortunately I made a good decision.

Off to New Orleans I ran as fast as my wayward feet could carry me, not realizing the pain I would cause my Mama, only knowing if I didn't go, my spirit, my soul and my life would end one way or the other. When I arrived in this melting pot of humanity, filled with wonder and complete acceptance, fate destined my path to cross with one of the smartest, kindest and most gentle souls anyone could ask for as a friend. Greg Johnston, his family steeped in New Orleans history and his family home smack dab in the center of the French Quarter, a three-story mansion on Royal Street. Old money, richer than anyone I had ever seen, but filled with grace and charm, he saved me and ended up a short time later sending me home to my Mama. In fact, he became one of Mama's dearest friends for the rest of his life.

That time of my life comes under the heading, "Hard Knock Life" long before the musical "Annie" coined an unforgettable song from childhood adversity. A story best left untold except for one thing, Jardin de L'Esprit. Sitting on Mr. Johnston's balcony one sunny July morning not long after my arrival, he told me he had called my Mama, and he was going to escort me home. He told me my Mama was beside herself with worry, and I couldn't run away from trouble. I simply had to face it and learn. I started crying like a spoiled brat. He shook his head and said, "Like I told your Mama and I'm telling you, when life gets this tough, shut your eyes and retreat into imagination for answers and solace. Jardin de L'Esprit, let the garden of your mind protect you." He went on, "It saved me all my long years and it will save you too."

So home I went to the loving arms of my Mama, her hair now actually gray at the temples from worry. Her new found love for Mr. Johnston and his life lesson saved her sanity, her baby boy and indeed her life.

From that day on when faced with sorrow, hatred, bigotry or any one of a hundred mind-numbing bruises, my Mama and I would look at each other, sigh and say our New Orleans mantra, "Jardin de L'Esprit". In fact, when Mama passed and I was standing alone amongst her wilting funeral flowers, I repeated this and my soul bloomed just enough that I could go on without her by my side.

If life hurts you in any number of ways, shut your eyes, sigh once then twice and visit your garden of the mind. My Mama's life lesson and Mr. Johnston's long ago lifesaver will protect you too.

Oh my, my coffee's cold and there's nothing worse than cold chicory...

Life Lesson #5

Miss Cassie's Countdown

Coming in from helping my Dad in the fields as a teenager, I found my Mama sitting at the big dining room table wiping tears from her eyes. I could hear her apparently talking to herself and what I heard was chilling to say the least. She repeated several times, "5, 4, 3, 2, 1, I'm on to the next world, Lilly. I've won."

I slowly walked through the partially opened sliding doors into that dining room, reserved for holidays and special occasions only. I was wide-eyed and trembling. It was cold in there, not normal for the middle of July, especially since the old farm house didn't have air conditioning. Focusing on my entry, Mama smiled and patted the chair next to her for me to sit. Once seated, she touched my arm and with her eyes sparkling said, "My son, Mama's fine so put that worried look away and let me tell you a story, a story about a strong courageous woman who bravely faced many trials in her lifetime and has now won glory, transitioning into eternity. Miss Cassie Arnold, my mentor and my confidante, my friend and my family."

Now perhaps it was my imagination but when Mama said Miss Cassie's name, it seemed the cold lifted in that quiet room, the sun shown through the tiny dust particles drifting in the light from the window next to the fireplace, and even the sound of the case clock on the mantle could be heard again, ticking in unison to my heartbeat. As the tale my Mama shared with me unfolded, I was transported to a time long before I was even a thought. Time truly is relative, and Mama's words made the journey backward as easy as sliding down the rabbit hole in "Alice in Wonderland."

Mama took a deep breath and continued her narrative. This is what she confided in me as best I can remember: "Miss Cassie Arnold, quite the character in the small town of Smyrna, Tennessee, lived just off the railroad tracks under the big Elm and Oak trees on Rock Springs Road, very close to where it changes names to Front Street, where now stands the Elders Chapel Church, and within a stone's throw of Hart's Branch Creek. Miss Cassie walked everywhere she went, driving an automobile just wasn't for her, and it seemed neither were shoes, as she marched through the year barefoot except in the coldest Winter months when a pair of worn men's army boots appeared from her closet, protecting her little feet from freezing. You could always tell though when Miss Cassie walked in the snow. Both soles of her army boots were cracked and made identifying her footprints as easy as those of a red fox.

Miss Cassie served the town as a midwife when needed, birthing for just about every family who couldn't afford a fancy doctor, serving freely and happily, never expecting any payment. Payment was always given though, sometimes in the form of food or firewood, used furniture or maintenance on her tiny house. Thus, she made a living, albeit meager, but a living nonetheless. Some families in Smyrna, often the rich and arrogant, tended to shun Miss Cassie, calling her crazy or a witch, mad or demented. They often laughed at her mismatched clothes and rolled their eyes as she pad footed along, sometimes even crossing the street to stay out of her path. Her clothes were indeed mismatched, but always clean and free of wrinkles, pressed neatly with a hot iron from her fireplace, unlike some of those high and mighty who looked down on her.

Miss Cassie worked tirelessly her whole life, caring for those less fortunate, including the many animals roaming her property, animals cast out by many of those same rich families because they no longer served a purpose. She tended her flock like some kind of patient prophet and could often be heard singing as she walked, or counting." I raised my eyebrows and opened my mouth to question when Mama interjected, "Yes, counting. Counting was her mantra, like – 1, 2, 3, 4, out the door. 5, 6, 7, 8, through the gate. 9, 10, move little hen; Miss Cassie's on her way to birth a child this day. On and on every day, no matter where she was. This was Miss Cassie's way. It was her way of talking, funny to some and maddening to others. But magical as well and soothing poetry to expectant mothers and those she helped. Even, 1, 2, 3, I'll bandage that knee, or 4, 5, 6, that rip I'll stitch. Her sad but favorite was 5, 6, 7, he's gone on to Heaven, spoken for babies, the elderly or any animal as life's breath left them."

Mama's story completely consumed my mind as I walked with Miss Cassie or waded into the creek with her based solely on my Mama's spoken word. I hadn't even noticed that Mama had poured me a glass of sweet tea until the ice popped, cracking in the syrupy mixture, breaking my reverie. When I looked up my Mama was watching me intently and continued, "Miss Cassie's good deeds went unnoticed by some, even when she jumped into that flooded Hart's Branch, saving the daughter of the local banker and cutting her little bare feet in the process on the rocks at the bank of the swollen creek. Even as she pulled that little sweet girl to safety, the rich banker snatched his daughter from Miss Cassie as if somehow saving her wasn't the point; the point was to get her away from the crazy old witch, instead of thanking her for her selfless act. A crowd had gathered at the creek's edge though, seeing Miss Cassie bobbing up and down in the water, and when she pulled that child to safety, cheers and applause erupted. Miss Cassie's only words were 1, 2, 3, now we'll see, this baby's safe and loved by me. As good deeds go though, it was soon forgotten and became just another chapter in Miss Cassie's book of good deeds, her book of life if you will."

Mama stopped her tale, putting her hand to her breast, and sighed a long sad sigh. I touched Mama's other hand and whispered, "Whatever happened to Miss Cassie?" Mama smiled and looking past me out the window to the sun, she said, "She passed away in her sleep this very day many years ago. I miss her every day and on this anniversary of her passing, her spirit just visited me this morning and said, '5, 4, 3, 2, 1, I'm on to the next world, Lilly. I've won. 10, 9, 8, at Heaven's gate I'll wait. Catch up, Lilly, don't be late.'" I hugged my Mama tight and I heard her quietly affirm, "See you soon, my friend, 4, 3, 2, I truly love you."

Now whether or not you believe in spirits, a good life and good deeds never go completely unnoticed. You can make a difference in this world just like Miss Cassie Arnold's countdown. Show love and respect to everyone around you and you'll be "3, 2, 1, on to the next world. Yes, you've won."

Life Lesson #6

Cleaning and Dreaming

Texting with my best friends today, I was bouncing my plans off them for publishing my book this year, a dream I've toyed with for a long time and been encouraged by many. Some roadblock has always managed to pop up to prevent it though, finances, health, personal relationships, work, births, deaths… just time in general I suppose.

Laughing with the girls on the phone and talking about how I should open my next Life Lesson, one of my friends suggested," When I awoke from a snowy night's sleep with a dream on my mind…" And true to normal for me, from the sweet memories of my Mama hiding in my old brain, this life lesson emerged, Cleaning and Dreaming.

One of the best times when I was small, long before school days took me away from spending all my time with Mama, was on Mondays. Mondays my Mama washed clothes, after the bus took the big kids to school and Daddy went to work or to the fields after a full night shift depending on his schedule. On Mondays Mama would wash. Using an old wringer-type washer and two metal wash tubs on the back porch for rinsing. (I'm sure if you don't know what a wringer washer is, then you've never stuck your arm through the wringer on a dare from your sister. Well, don't. I did and trust me, just search history on wringer washer instead. It's easier, safer and far less painful, especially listening to your sister laugh afterward. Another story for that later on.)

Mama would wash, push them through the ringer, rinse and repeat. Seemingly monotonous but therapeutic in a fashion I suppose. She'd wash and sing, at the same time keeping an eye on me in the backyard with the dogs, the geese and the calf in the kitchen garden out behind the clothesline. Oh yes, a clothesline. No fancy dryer for us back then, only a clothesline, a sunny windy day and, of course, my Mama's imagination. That particular wash day was sheets, towels and white things. All were washed, rinsed wrung out and carried in the big clothes basket to the line. Me in tow, hanging by one hand to Mama's dress tail and pulling the dog along by her collar. What a parade we made!

I asked Mama what she was doing and she said, "Honey I'm cleaning and dreaming. You want to help?" Immediately letting go of the dog (happily running off to chase the geese) and letting go of Mama's dress. I shook my head with a definite, "Yes ma'am!" And so the dream that day began. Mama hung the sheets and towels and from the ends of the short towels she clothes pinned Daddy's t-shirts. From a distance it looked like to my child's eye that a fort was forming. Mama was taking her cleaning chores and turning them into an imaginative dream just for us.

All day we played in that fort, running back and forth through t-shirt windows, out towel doors and protected by walls of pure white cotton sheets, all flapping in that summer breeze. My Mama singing and laughing and chasing me in and around until every piece of her laundry chores was dry. Then as she dismantled that cotton fort, she told me stories of her childhood. A whole day of stories and fun. And love.

When we were done and all that laundry folded, Mama grabbed me up and swung me around by my outstretched arms, me screaming and laughing. She hugged me tight and whispered in my ear, "Little one, never grow too old for cleaning and dreaming. If you have a heartbeat, there's still time for dreaming."

Almost 50 years to the day after washing clothes on that back porch, my sweet little Mama, no longer able to walk, sound asleep in her chair, snoring away, I stood and watched her, not knowing she only had a few months to keep me company, and as I watched her sleeping, breath labored with age, a sweet smile crossed her face, and she whispered in her sleep laughing, "Little sir, you come back here..." Yes, still dreaming, cleaning her memories and dreaming, cleaning and dreaming. A tear ran down my cheek and

I patted her little face, making sure she was warm and covered. I thought of that day years before and the sheets flapping in the breeze, so clean and fresh. Yes, Mama, if you have a heartbeat there's still time for dreams and just perhaps... even beyond this life, a dream yet awaits.

Life Lessons #7 and #8

Two for the Price of One

Another 4th of July is upon us. Another national birthday party. You'd think that would draw us closer together, right? After all, we can't blow out the candles on a 241-year old birthday cake if we all don't get together to do it. Ok, ok, I won't turn this Life Lesson into a political rant, but I remembered over coffee this morning something my Mama tried to teach me long ago, very relevant today.

My Mama loved paying bills. Not that she loved owing money, but if she owed, she loved paying. Mama took great care in marking down every payment and great pride when she walked out of a business or a bank with a paid-off note in her hand. On one such occasion, I remember Mama standing at the teller's window of our town's small bank, waiting somewhat patiently to make the final payment of a long-standing loan. The tellers were taking their time, gossiping about every customer as they left the bank (this one was always late paying, that one owed everyone in town, that type of mean-spirited gossip).

As she waited and listened, Mama's little foot started tapping, slowly at first, finally machine gun paced. I could feel the tension… the tellers had no idea that they were about to get hit by the wrath of Hurricane Lillian. Finally, Mama had her original note in hand and we turned to leave. I let out a sigh of relief, knowing they were spared by the Grace of God, when it struck!!

With her back to the teller cages, Mama said in a sweet Southern voice, albeit loud and to the point, "Ladies…" The place got quiet, conversation stopped and business halted. Mama turned and placed her gloved hand lightly on the customer service sign and smiled. "Standing here listening to your conversation, I found such a good recipe for drama. You… You're at least a cup of gossip, and you…

You supplied a good half cup of rumors. And my dear, you're at least a pound of jealousy. Why, if you mix all that up well and cover it with lies, roast it for as long as you lack self-esteem, you ought to eat well tonight." Mouths dropped open, customers snickered, and we walked out, never to bank there again.

I started laughing and congratulating Mama on her judgment, when she stopped, got that twinkle in her eye and said, "Son, don't ever judge someone because they sin differently than you." And with that said, I'll leave you to your national birthday celebrations just like my Mama left me on that day long ago, Life Lessons, two for the price of one.

Life Lesson #9

❦

Civilization, Paint and Whitewash

O nce while sitting on my stoop, the New Orleans version of a front porch, I happened to hear a wandering couple's far from complimentary commentary on Southern life. With the faint sound of an impromptu jazz band floating up from Jackson Square like fine river mist, my sweet Southern reverie was broken and I felt my mouth open in an attempt to channel a lesson from my Mama, a lesson I had heard my Mama give some 50 years prior.

One very warm day in April 1961, I stood with Mama outside the tiny grocery store at Hilltop, a little community sandwiched between Smyrna and LaVergne, Tennessee, when up pulled a very fancy Cadillac with out of state license plates. Down came the passenger's power window and a snobby little nasal voice said, "Honey, I realize you local yokels don't travel much but could you point us to civilization?" My Mama tensed slightly but smiling sweetly, she began to teach.

"Ma'am, I don't need to travel too far from my door to recognize rudeness when I hear it. Here in the civilized South, we've birthed the likes of William Faulkner, Truman Capote, Eudora Welty and Robert Penn Warren. Let me recommend you buy a copy of Harper Lee's novel <u>To Kill a Mockingbird</u>, another civilized Southern work." Mama then went on to say, "Quoting Miss Lee, people generally see what they look for and hear what they listen for. Indeed, what I see and what I hear is uneducated bigotry. Civilization is about 40 miles back to the North, ma'am."

The Cadillac lady's brightly painted lips dropped open and as the window started back up, Mama said, "Too poor to paint and too proud to whitewash, y'all come back now." Mama turned without hesitation and off down the rock road we walked hand in hand, proud to be right where we belonged.

Watching the current reincarnated nasal voice couple meander off down my French Quarter street, and remembering my Mama's lesson, I could only smile and say, "Y'all come back now, I'm whitewashing my gate later on. Bring a brush."

The moment for channeling passed and even though my attempt to thwart rude behavior paled in comparison to my Mama's so many years before, I felt better about myself. At the end of the day, isn't that self worth a treasure we all need nowadays? Never be afraid to speak up for your beliefs, rich or poor, paint or whitewash.

Life Lesson #10

Final Destination

With all the bitterness, hate, mistrust and division in our nation lately, I find myself remembering a simpler time, a time when my Mama taught a young boy about brotherhood and trust.

Summer vacation 1963 was upon us, that final school bell rang for my third grade class, and we were out the door faster than squirrels. Down the steps and into the road, heads turning from right to left looking for mischief. We had three months before fourth grade locked us back into our classrooms, and we were going to change the world before then. Alas, after three weeks we had done everything our little brains had concocted during the school year, and we sat in the hay loft, feet dangling out the big double doors, scanning the horizon for something to occupy us.

In the distance we could see my Mama, apron flapping in the breeze, gliding down the path between the chicken house and our barn refuge. Carrying lovingly prepared sack lunches, Mama was pulling a brightly painted wooden box on wheels. A box on wheels... now that was something we hadn't seen. We all looked wide-eyed from one to another and we scrambled down the ladder to the ground, arriving the same moment Mama walked up in front of the barn, box in tow.

"Sit down children," she began, "let's see how we can get into a summer adventure. This box contains hidden treasure, precious and never ending." The excitement at fever pitch we edged closer to the box, noticing but not caring the box was poorly painted really and the wheels were some old Red Flyer wheels my Daddy had discarded months back. Mama continued, "I'm going to take this box into the fields and when I return, get ready for the finest treasure hunt your little heads can imagine."

And with that said, off she went through the corn field, up over the hill, disappearing into the cedar thicket at the back of our property. Not long after, we saw Mama pop back out of the thicket minus the treasure chest, wiping her hands on that billowy apron and almost skipping back to our location. "Gather round Pirates," she called out as she plopped down on a painted tractor tire planted with roses, "let's begin."

She started weaving our fantasy, a plan for each of us to become richer and richer as the summer unfolded. We had to follow her instruction to get the reward and if we didn't, the treasure would never be found, lost forever in that dark sweet smelling cedar thicket. We were tasked with figuring out how to build a tractor-sized road across the fields over the hill and to that cedar thicket using only our hands and a few small tools from the shed. Only when we finished that road, and Daddy could get the tractor to the thicket would we get our treasure. So the Pirate Treasure Road Adventure began.

We cut, we dug, we piled rocks along the edge of our road, and day by day, week by week, our road took shape. Right along the corn field, over the hill, through the orchard and right to the edge of that cedar thicket. By the third week in August we had reached our goal and behind us down that dusty rock edged road came Daddy driving his tractor. Perched behind him, her tiny hands hooked in the straps of his overalls, was Mama smiling from ear to ear. That tractor smoking and clanking made its way right to the thicket, and we all cheered. Treasure awaited us and we had worked hard for it.

Daddy lifted Mama down like a fairy princess or a china doll and into the thicket she disappeared. Shortly she emerged wiping her now dirty hands on that same apron, the chest no worse for wear creaked behind her on wheels unused for a couple of months. As we breathlessly awaited our treasure, Mama opened the box and pulled out a hand sewn bag made from a flour sack, far too small to hold riches. She opened it and pulled from the depths four silver dollars and placed one in each of our hands. Needless to say, we stood silent. All that work for this?

Mama saw our confusion and wiping away a small tear, she said, "My children, the treasure is already in you. Look at your strong arms from building, look at your tan faces from being out in the sun and clean air. Even better, look at the trust and friendship you've built this summer. God blessed you with such treasure. Know that your situation is not your final destination. The best is yet to come." Daddy lifted her sweetly back up behind him and the tractor labored back down our treasure road, hand built with love and determination.

I just today pulled out a small stone I've saved from the remnants of that magnificent testament to brotherhood, that road to adventure, and I can hear my Mama singing in Heaven.

Just know the best is yet to come. Let's all pull together and build a road through confusion and adversity. Treasure awaits.

Life Lesson #11

Baggage

Now that I'm retired I find I'm watching more reality television, not the most intellectually challenging retirement perhaps but it is giving me just a bit of time to settle into something worthwhile. I keep hearing a recurring statement resonating through the themes, "He has too much baggage for me." As if this is a proud statement invented by the younger generation, I find myself smiling a "Mama Smile." Ignoring the tongue ring and multiple nose rings and earrings on the current reality show participant, I am taken back to my college days. Coming home from classes one lazy October day, my Mama inquired about my current love interest as she often did, and I shrugged my shoulders, mumbling "too much baggage." Thinking I had outsmarted my Mama with a new generational idea, I distinctly remember my Mama turning her head down so she could serenely look over her glasses, paused in mid look and said, "Everyone comes with baggage, baby, the challenge is finding someone who loves you enough to help you unpack your own." With that she pushed the glasses back to their normal position and silently moved on to the next subject at hand, leaving me, mouth open, pondering my predicament.

So on this lazy afternoon I'll leave you with a fully packed bag and pray you find your own unpacked love interest my friends. Wonder how I'd look with a nose ring... no, I think not.

Life Lesson #12

Tick Tock

At an intersection this morning waiting for the light to change, I started noticing the people around me. The overly-painted Subaru lady next to me had tears rolling down her cheeks, the Mac truck guy beyond her chomping on a cigar had eyes blazing with anger. In front of me, her head bobbing to ear-bud music, a teenager laughed, her Kia Soul bouncing like her head, and finally rambling through the intersection in a big old Cadillac, was a little blue-haired jewel, barely able to see through her steering wheel, a long thin cigarette dangling from her ruby red lips. All these people going about their daily routine, completely unaware of each other. The light changed and we all moved on, but at that moment I realized each one of those people affected and changed my journey just by being there at that intersection. We are not alone. Every decision we make, every experience we have changes the universal clock, the minute hand changing with every tick, every tock. With cancer knocking at my door every day, financial woes standing at the window and lost love staring back at me from the mirror, I find it difficult to keep going. We all have bad days, we truly do.

I am reminded of a November day in 1987, finding my Daddy after his suicide, I thought my life was over. At his funeral, my little Mama put aside her own anguish, held my face in her trembling hands and said, "Baby, the past is where you learned lessons, the future is where you will teach others based on those lessons, so don't stop now in the middle. When you think you've come to the end of your rope, tie a knot in it and hang on."

The lesson today is that the clock keeps ticking. You never know how you can affect someone else's journey just by being you. Having each of you in my life changes my path every day. Thank you for that. Let's see what changes are in store for us today my friends.

Life Lesson #13

Book of Life

We all know that one of the joys of a high school student is the prom, right? The whole process, picking out your date, squirreling up the courage to ask, choosing and re-choosing what you'll wear, and how you'll get there, even washing your old truck until the paint is so thin you can see the metal (yea, I actually did that). Of course, we can't forget staying up late and the dancing. Well, my friends, for those of you lucky enough to have been raised in a religion that frowns on dancing, let alone other personality quirks, the next part of my story will bring back memories for sure.

As the prom rolled around my Junior year, the leaders of our congregation began to feverishly preach on the sins of close body contact dancing. At the time I'm thinking a little close body contact was holding hands and kissing but dancing might be in proximity. When our preacher and the elders found out I was going to the prom, they paid a visit to our house to discuss my sinful upbringing with my Mama and Daddy.

Sitting between my parents, I could tell they were listening intently as these men preached fire and brimstone right there on our Naugahyde sofa. That couch was smoking by the time the sermon was finished. I glanced at Mama to see what the outcome was going to be, only to find her looking straight at me. She winked, and I knew we were in for a "Mama Sermon". She had my back.

Mama stood up, straightened her apron, walked to the screen door and opened it wide. Turning to her guests, she said, "Gentlemen, in the Book of Life, everybody has a chapter they don't read out loud. I doubt God will fault me for not reading this one any further. Good day." And with that I not only danced at the prom but my soul has been dancing ever since.

So if your Book of Life is missing something, it's all good. A new chapter is simply a page away, and you may want to read it out loud… or not.

Life Lesson #14

Taken for Granted

Walking the streets of New Orleans in the Fall means clear blue sky peaking between centuries old buildings. The air is crisp and somewhat clean, albeit not as sweet as a Tennessee hillside but remember you'd smell funny too if you were almost 300 years old.

Street vendors setting up for the day's business, locals stopping at every open door to check on friends, and tourists who haven't yet slept from the night before stumbling aimlessly trying to remember exactly where their hotel is. Not quite the Fall memories from a Tennessee perspective, but as you can imagine, it's all relative.

With all that said, I am reminded of some advice my little Mama gave me one Fall morning rocking away on her porch, her little glasses dangling from the pearl chain around her neck. For no reason whatsoever that rocker stopped, she squeezed my hand and said, "The things you take for granted, someone else is praying for." I opened my mouth to speak, but her eyes sparkled in true "Mama" fashion and with the clack of her rocker going again, no retort from me was needed and none had better be forthcoming. Just learn, and I did.

On this first day of Fall, think about my Mama's words. Never take anything for granted, Someone else may snap it up with one small prayer. I love you.

Life Lesson #15

Proud

Sitting watching a bike race today, I heard shouts of "Make your Daddy proud," and from another, "Make your Mama proud." I even heard a couple shouts of, "That's no way to make me proud, try harder." I smiled to myself thinking back to shortly after my little Mama passed away. I started the difficult and emotional task of packing up her things on the table beside her chair and I chanced to open a small calendar type notebook. Mama was as organized as they come. This little notebook was filled with appointments, lists, to do's and quotes for the day. In her little hen-scratched writing on almost every page was this note, "I'm going to make you proud today – note to self." Mama knew the main person (other than God) to make proud is yourself. If you've done that, you've far outstretched any other opinion. And looking back, there was never a day I wasn't proud of my Mama, and that holds true long after her passing.

Definitely make yourself proud of you, and others will follow, or not. And if they don't, well, just make that as a "note to self" as well.

Life Lesson #16

Gumbo

Starting a pot of gumbo this fine October morning, the smells mingled in my tiny kitchen. As my concoction bubbled away, a little advice from my Mama crept out of my memory, and as is normal for me, I needed to share it.

Mama said one Fall morning long ago when I had questioned her on how to deal with some problem, now forgotten, "Act your way through it my baby. Acting is the ability to dream on cue. Your dreams become reality little by little. Absorb the characters around you like a good gumbo, pepper it with a little of your own experience and the play of life will be as exciting for the actor as the audience. Life is nothing more than a true bowl of soul at any rate so embrace the diversity."

Now exactly how this applies to your fine morning, I'll leave up to you. Perhaps nothing more than a tiny bit of "Mama Wisdom". Use it, or discard it, but look at yourself, and enjoy the gumbo you call life, the life each of you has created. Smile often and feel the excitement of a new day.

I think my gumbo needs a little more cayenne...

Life Lesson #17

Say What

Every Saturday at 10 a.m. like clockwork my Mama went to the Beauty Shop. Not a Salon but an honest-to-goodness beauty shop, curlers, sit-under hair dryers, and teased hair pressed flat on the back by Monday because she slept on it.

One Saturday during a particularly brutal hair teasing session, the local town gossip sat in the chair next to Mama and began to discuss one of her friends' sex life. The details were lurid and raunchy. Mama got more and more uncomfortable by the minute, meaning her temper was beginning to flare and a Momism was forming in her tightly "teased" head.

At the height of the gossip rampage, Mama turned to the lady and said, "Honey, I'm sure if you'll discuss your friend with us, you'll discuss us with your friend so tighten your lip like your curlers and move one chair over." The lady moved, the rampage stopped, Mama's hair was teased and combed out and all was right with the world.

If you want your private life private, tighten your curlers and honor a friend's trust. This man doesn't have a hair to tease and I guess that's a good thing.

Life Lesson #18

Let the Spirit Take You

On this Labor Day when all is quiet in a city not known for calm, I'm reminded of one day long ago when after picking beans all day, our backs bent over, sore, tired and dirty, my Mama all of a sudden dropped her bucket of beans, straightened her back, stretched her arms to the sky, let out the biggest laugh and began to dance, no music, just dancing and laughing. I thought, ok she's finally lost her mind and I better go get Daddy off the tractor. After all, I had already learned my Mama was a little out there from time to time. This time though she had as my Granny used to say, "tipped the coffee into the saucer".

Wide-eyed I began to slowly back away down that bean row, and my Mama stopped and said, "Honey, Mama's not crazy, I'm just feeling life till my skin tingles. There's so much real life and happiness in my soul that sometimes you just have to let the Spirit take you."

Well, Mama's laugh was so contagious my feet started moving, my hands starting lifting up and before I knew it, I was dancing along with her in that hot country bean field. Happiness took me too and I laughed till my sides hurt.

Truly remember, happiness is just a tingle away. This old man feels a dance in his soul, don't you?

Life Lesson #19

Heartbeat

T he morning of November 23, 1963, our nation awoke to a sadness and emptiness we weren't ready to acknowledge. The loss of our President the day before and the loss of our collective innocence from the family years of the 50's was a turning point for all of us.

When I woke up that morning in Smyrna, Tennessee, my Mama was cooking breakfast. I could smell the sausage and hear the popping from the fire in the wood stove in my room. Mama had of course gotten up early to light every fire in the house to make sure her family was cozy and warm.

After a quiet somber breakfast and right before I was supposed to catch the bus to school, my Mama took my hand. Out past the old white barn we walked hand in hand, Mama humming softly to herself, a sad smile on her face but an ever increasingly tight grip on my hand. Knowing I would probably miss my bus to school I began to fidget, but never said a word. When Mama was on a mission, I learned argument was useless.

We walked and walked, past the barn, past the remnants of summer corn, all the way to the far corner of our property. When we reached the last old rusted fence, Mama turned to face me. She pulled my little hand to her breast and said, "Baby boy, feel my heartbeat. Now feel your own chest. That same strong beat is part of me. There will come a time when you'll stand here on your own, a grown man, and you'll be lonely or sad, anxious or mad, troubled or even excited and full of love. Whenever the day, whatever the time, however you come to this spot, you put that sweet little hand over your heart and I am here with you. That heartbeat is me inside you for as long as it beats. She turned, hugged me and back down the dew covered path to the house we went.

Recently, I stood in that same spot, sadly surrounded by the interstate and a fancy subdivision now. While drivers drove by wondering, an old man stood there with his shaking hand on his heart, tears streaming down through the wrinkles. I felt whole, at peace and my soul was strong. I love you Mama and I love everyone who takes the time to read this.

Put your hand over your heart. That beat lets you know you're never really alone. If you think you have no one, you always have this old man as your friend. That has to count for something.

Life Lesson #20

God's Tears

As I watched the rain drops dripping off my Mama's roses this morning in the garden, I remembered her telling me when I was very young how "God's tears washed everything clean," and she used the rain dripping off these very roses to picture it in my mind. She'd say, "Baby, look at how the roses bow their heads thanking God for His rain. After the rain, they'll raise their heads in praise to the Sun."

Climbing on her lap as she rocked away, in my childlike innocence I told her I would cut some of them and bring them to her grave. I'm not sure where that sentiment came from but up and out of a child's mouth. My Mama patted my head and said, "Honey, let's make sure and enjoy them now while Mama is here with you. And with a tight hug Mama rocked me to sleep in her lap, humming a soothing melody. I vividly remember as my eyes closed, the last sight I saw were the roses as they raised their heads for the sun. Every Mother's Day now I take a few of them as I promised I would to honor her memory, knowing she's still here with me to enjoy them. I sure miss her voice though.

A bitter sweet good night. Tomorrow is a new day with new hopes and challenges, and new blooms on my roses.

Life Lesson #21

Acceptance

Sitting at my new favorite camping spot, I realized alone time can sure clear your head of the drama surrounding any unanswered questions. Thinking back over the many questions I've asked myself and others over the years, I happened upon an event that happened in my college life, something truly only my Mama could teach me.

Graduating from college, I remember walking across the stage to receive my diploma and hearing my Mama's voice yelling in the vast crowd of the auditorium/gymnasium. She sounded happier, and louder, than any member of that group, and with good reason I guess since it took me a year or so longer than most to get my degree. Along the way I had changed my major and minors several times. I just couldn't make up my mind what I wanted to do with my life. Often I would seek Mama's advice through my college years, and she was always happy to give it. Once though I had so many questions about an issue that Mama just hugged me tight and said, "Breathe, my son, slow down and take a breath. The answers to everything are in your head already, or your heart. If you can't find answers there, well then you may have to realize some questions don't need answers and quite frankly some never need to be asked."

As I held my diploma tight to my chest and a wave of both relief and pride covered me, I looked out into that crowd. Seeing Mama on her feet waving both arms high above her head, still gripping her little "old lady" purse in one hand, I knew my path was the right one. I had chosen perfectly for that moment in time, and if I didn't have all the answers, well, perhaps letting go of the questions was indeed the only answer for now. I kissed one finger and pointed to my Mama far out into that crowd and placed my hand over my heart. Mama crossed her arms over her heart in response and even though she was far away in that sea of people, she and I both knew she too walked across that stage with me. She continues to travel with me every day, answering questions in my head or reminding me to breathe and let go.

So if you can't seem to find an answer to whatever problems that surround you, learn a lesson from my Mama. Simply let go. Acceptance may be the best answer ever.

Life Lesson #22

Monologue

My Mama told me something at 16 when she found me in the barn moping over my then current love interest who had started dating my best friend. She said, "Baby, when a relationship becomes a monologue, it's time to find real conversation." After all these years I figured it out.

Who knew… have a good day children and here's hoping you have conversation in your life.

Life Lesson #23

Perception of Troubles

Perception of Troubles vs blessings. When I was probably no more than 3 or 4, I remember my Daddy and Mama carrying me through a hot cornfield, the rows were tight and claustrophobic, and heavily planted with morning glory vines to draw insects and bees away from the ears of corn.

Carrying me through the hot corn rows, my Daddy suddenly lifted my head above the corn and the breeze was amazing, but the real perception change came as I watched a sea of blue flowers dancing on top of the corn. I shouted, "Look Daddy, the ocean."

Perception depends on timing, position and sometimes a strong arm from a friend lifting you above your troubles. Never doubt perception can change in an instant.

Life Lesson #24

Fear is Temporary

The sermon in church one Sunday long ago was "Fear is Temporary, Regret lasts Forever." Now to a boy of 10 that had to mean God was telling me to go right out after church to the old rock quarry and make that 25 foot jump into the dark cold water at the bottom. How I came to that decision is a mystery to me now, but remember I was 10.

So after church I found myself in my tighty whities standing at the edge of the quarry staring down at that dark water. Hearing the preacher's voice from that morning, I counted to 3 and took my leap of faith.

The freefall was exhilarating, the belly flop not so much. After what seemed like forever I surfaced. I had conquered my fear and would never regret trying. God was right!

Then I saw my Mama on the edge looking down at me in the water. The look on her face let me know a new fear/regret scenario was unfolding...my Mama whipped my tighty whities all the way back to the house.

This Life Lesson is definitely listen to God but know that everything is open to interpretation, especially at 10 years old.

Life Lesson #25

Duck and Cover

I'm told (and prayerfully no one will slap me with a you-were-there) that in the late 50's children were being taught to "duck and cover" in case of an atomic bomb, to hide themselves, protect their heads, etc. Now what good that would do in an atomic explosion you tell me, but it was all they (we) had.

Coming home from school scared and telling my realist Mama what I had learned, she just laughed. She told me, "My baby, if you learn to duck and cover, you learn that for all bad things in life, duck and cover your little head from all hurt and don't you cry cause Mama will be there to pat your safe little head every time."

No matter what hurt I've had be it physical, or even a broken heart, I feel that little pat on my old bald head. So duck and cover today, and if you feel a little pat on your head, well, that just might be me sending you a little love from a friend.

Life Lesson #26

❦

Age Limit on Dreams

Never put an age limit on your dreams. As a single person, aging can be a scary thing. Choices have to be made and pathways taken, but uncomfortable or not, they're all just avenues to fulfilling whatever dreams you've hoped for.

My Mama didn't get out often in the last few years before she passed, whether it was because her joints hurt or it was difficult to get her up and ready. Perhaps dealing with the wheelchair took too much effort, or it simply could have been nothing more than she had decided the comfort of her home and the warmth of her recliner outweighed whatever waited in the open world. Some days though, we would gather her things, pack the wheelchair and simply explore! We might shop, we might eat at a restaurant or we might just drive through the countryside, her little eyes dancing from one scene to the next.

On one of these outings we chanced upon a young Mom and Dad at a fast food establishment. They had a small child who was all over the place, laughing, talking, running and blatantly being exactly what she was – a child. The parents tried to curtail her and keenly aware that most customers were annoyed, they did their best to corral her to a general three-booth containment. Our booth just happened to be one of the three containment centers, right next to them in fact.

I saw Mama laughing and talking to the little girl. Thinking she might be tired or at best weary, I suggested we continue on our journey. Mama shook her head as the little girl brought a toy to her for Mama to inspect. The child immediately climbed onto Mama's lap, the wheelchair groaned and slipped backward. I reached for Mama at the same time the parents reached for their child. Mama just laughed out loud and hugged that baby girl tight.

As the parents profusely apologized, my sweet Mama proclaimed, "What a blessing you have in your daughter. Children don't move, think or speak in a straight line, and neither does imagination, nor creativity. Children see magic in everything and everyone because they look for it. Let them look, watch them closely though, and love them fiercely." That little baby kissed Mama on the cheek and was down and off about her play.

Both parents hugged Mama, and I could tell her lesson had made an impression. As I cleaned our table and started pushing the wheelchair toward the door, the Mother waved goodbye to us with a tear in her eye. None of us ever saw each other again, but I often wonder what adventures that tiny child had over the years. When we got all packed back in the car, Mama said, "Son, keep the wonder of a child when you open a new door. You just never know who or what is waiting."

What doorway will you face today? There is no age limit on dreams. Why, some day you may get old enough to start reading fairy tales again.

Life Lesson #27

Nap Time

Nap Time may be overrated. As a child, nap time on a floor pallet with my Mama was an adventure. The big kids off at school, my Mama was all mine and before I drifted off to sleep she told me wonderful stories to spark truly imaginative dreams.

Well, with writer's block looming, I decided to see if nap time would excite my imagination to create some awesome new stories. I should have realized when I couldn't remember exactly what a pallet was that nap time isn't the same at my age. Once I Googled "pallet" I had to actually get down on the floor to utilize my creation. Mistake. Once down knowing it was going to take Life Alert to get me back up, I had to use my phone to find someone to tell me imaginative stories. Now my friends, 800 numbers are imaginative but not quite the stories I was looking for.

After all that, I never went to sleep. I'm still lying here debating on how to get up, but I did find a new story through all this. Nap time may be overrated, but stories never are. Sleep well my children. My pallet needs some TLC

Life Lesson #28

Get Direction

I'm one of those people who can get lost even with the best GPS. Either I don't listen, completely ignoring the annoying GPS lady or I simply worry too much about what's coming up next, that I completely ignore the turn right now.

Sadly, I have asked for direction in the past. My acting coach simply told me "do something different." Now seriously, how can I do something different if I don't know sort of where I'm going to begin with. I have a friend who recently told me he didn't have time to give me direction, being busier than any human should be, but the best one was my Mom. I once asked Mom during a particularly bad personal moment if she could help direct me to neutral ground. Mom's response was typical of her. She said, "Baby, God gives the direction, we just enforce it."

Next time you need direction, remember God is probably the only road sign worth following, so enforce that sign and you'll never be lost.

Life Lesson #29

Morning Light Makes It Right

Dreams for children (and ornery old men) can be scary to say the least, left over terrors from a bad experience the day before, or even as simple as overactive imagination. As we grow older, we pretty much recognize them for what they are, but every once in a while the Dream Monsters from our childhood can still play havoc late at night.

My Mama's answer for night terrors was a good drink of well water. She'd gather her baby in her arms and whisper, "Morning light will make it right, morning light will make it right." Drifting off to sleep with that mantra in my head, the Dream Monsters never won a battle.

As I opened my eyes this morning, after a night of fighting Dream Monsters, the morning light really did make it right or at least "rightable". Mama's mantra from all those years ago still protects her baby boy.

Try it and may this morning's light make your day right.

Life Lesson #30

What Does in Love Mean

W hat does "in love" mean? Growing up in a small town and under my Mama and Daddy meant basic learning, common sense, hard work, hard play, lots of discipline when needed, and good sleep. Basically, the kind of childhood every child deserves, but sadly many don't get nowadays.

I came home from school as a junior and had decided I was IN love and ready to settle down, but just to make sure I thought I better ask my Mama. So when I asked Mama the difference between loving and being in love, Mama looked hard into my eyes and said, "Son, in love is when the brain stops and the heart takes over. You'll try to eat cereal with a fork, put salt in your coffee, wear your shirt inside out and life will never be the same." Scared the crap out of me.

Well, turned out I wasn't IN love that time, but have truly been at least once since then. Only thing now is I think all those IN love attributes for me lately sound like simply old age and have nothing to do with brain, heart or being in love whatsoever. So, if you think you're in love my friends, just make sure it's not dementia; there are drugs for that. Good night, my children, this "in love" man is going to bed, if I can remember where it is.

Life Lesson #31

Imagination

I brought home a picture I had painted in 4th grade of a dancing purple bear. I was in tears because everyone had laughed saying there was no such thing. My Mama took me to the garden and showed me a caterpillar and said, "Baby, imagination will give that caterpillar wings in the form of a butterfly, and imagination is what made that beautiful purple bear dance. Nurture that, and imagination will make you travel when old legs won't walk."

Shortly before my Mama passed away and after she hadn't walked for years, I asked her why she seemed so content in her chair. She just smiled that sweet little smile and said in her hushed voice, "Baby, don't you remember, imagination has made me travel right here in my chair just like that caterpillar flew and your purple bear danced when you were small."

As I fall off to sleep tonight, I know there's a caterpillar flying and a purple bear dancing because my Mama believed in a child's imagination. Good night one and all, imagine what tomorrow will bring.

Life Lesson #32

Find New Laughter

After working really hard on a project recently I came to the realization my efforts were not only unappreciated but taken completely for granted. Surprise changed to anger then to simply hurt. To pull myself out of a negative place, I remembered something Mama taught me in my late high school years.

I had let a buddy on the football team cheat from a paper to make a passing grade, and he told everyone what a "patsy" I was. I told Mama, and she said, "Baby, a wise man sat in the audience and cracked a joke. Everybody laughed like crazy. After a moment he cracked the same joke again. This time less people laughed. He cracked the same joke again and again, and when there were no laughs he smiled and said, you can't laugh at the same joke again and again, so why keep crying over the same sadness over and over. Leave it to those who will and find new laughter.

So as the Robin sings the morning awake, I'll move on to find new laughter. My wish for you is sunshine, and fun. If you feel unappreciated by someone, leave them and travel on. I appreciate every one of you every day.

Life Lesson #33

Salty Coffee

S hortly before my Mama passed she shared a funny but poignant life lesson with a lady in our town. This lady couldn't decide if her husband was cheating on her or not, and she asked my Mama for advice. A very dangerous thing to do because as you can imagine, my Mama spoke her mind freely, especially when prompted by a question, any question in fact.

My Mama replied quickly and with conviction, 'Honey, the minute you start to wonder whether you can trust someone or not, that is when you know you don't. Keep your eyes open, even salt looks like sugar." That lady went on to meet someone else who loved and respected her, and I'm sure her coffee has been salt free to this day.

So, if you have any doubts today children, make sure to throw out the salty coffee. Sweetness is waiting for each of you.

Life Lesson #34

Every Seat Is Important

There was a time when you could ride the train from Smyrna to Nashville, Tennessee daily just like commuter bus service. Relaxing clickety clack along the rails watching pasture turn to city before your eyes. One October morning after the big kids went off to school my Mama decided she and I would spend the 50 cents and visit her sister on South 6th Street in the city.

We packed a snack, got a ride to the train station in Smyrna (Mama didn't drive), got a ticket, and I sat on the bench wide-eyed listening for the train whistle. Wasn't long and there she was, a huge engine, two cars and that wonderful little caboose, a Rockwell lover's dream. Life was about to change for me forever.

As we began to board at the front of the train, my Mama snatched me up and duck walked me to the last car and the last door. She handed the open mouthed porter our tickets, boarded the last car and we were seated. Several people asked us if we were lost and a few turned their heads and mumbled. Didn't phase me, I was riding a train. My Mama looked at me with tears in her eyes and said, "Son, every seat is important, learn this!"

When we got to Nashville and got off the train in the late 50's segregation, I was surrounded by people of color. My Mama stood proudly holding her tiny very white child in a perfect sea of black faces. Yes, every seat is important, Mama. Thank you.

Life Lesson #35

Bluntly Honest

People watching in Walmart the other day, I was reminded of one of my favorite "Momisms". "Just because they make it in your size doesn't mean you need to wear it." I'll leave that bluntly honest thought to each of you this morning as I change my jeans for the third time. I know I have another size in this closet somewhere.

Life Lesson #36

An Open Hand, a Basket of Eggs and a Bushel of Tomatoes

When I was a child, I used to scrap and fight all the time. One particular fight I almost lost my best friend, Steve Ryan. Steve lived across the field from my house on the next farm down the road. We had grown up together, our families farming side by side for years. A few hours after the fight, Steve came to our screen door and stuck his hand out for me to shake it and I shut the door.

My Mama, standing behind me in the living room, grabbed my hand and turned it palm up. She said, "Learn this lesson. An open hand means friendship or help and either one is worthy of respect." She kissed my hand and told me the choice was mine.

With that said, she went off to the kitchen and I went to the barn to ponder not only what she told me but why exactly my friend and I had been arguing anyway. I barely had time to climb the ladder to the loft when I heard Mama yelling my name from the back porch. Back down the ladder I went and quickly through the kitchen garden to the house steps. Mama was holding her egg basket and as I walked up, she pushed it toward me and said, "Son, Mrs. Ryan needs two dozen eggs so take these across the field to her pronto."

Mrs. Ryan was Steve's mother so that meant I was going to have to face him when I got to their house. My Mama's eyes glittered as I opened my mouth to object. Seeing that look on her face, and since there was no sound coming from me, Mama said, "Get going!" And going I did! Down the hill from our house and into the field separating our two farms. Emerging from the corn on the Ryan's side of the field, I could see Mrs. Ryan was waiting for me on their back porch. Mr.

Ryan was smoking his pipe in his chair, and their daughter, Julie Ann, was playing with her dolls on the steps. Steve was nowhere in sight. "Good," I thought, "I can deliver these eggs and hightail myself home without facing him right now."

Fate (and our two Mamas) would intervene. Mrs. Ryan thanked me for the eggs and told me there was a bushel basket of tomatoes in the barn to take back to my Mama for canning. She pointed toward the open barn door and without a thought, I meandered to their barn, two dogs and a farm cat following me along the way. I knew this was a contrived ambush the minute I walked through the door and saw my friend mucking out the horse stalls in the back – that bushel basket of tomatoes positioned on a work bench directly across from the stalls. He looked up, as surprised as I was, and after a very awkward few seconds, stuck out his hand again as I approached. This time my hand went out in unison, and we both started apologizing as we shook hands, friends once again. (As if our friendship had really ever been in jeopardy.)

Laughing, I started to head home, almost forgetting the tomatoes. When we walked out of the barn, I noticed his entire family standing together on the porch. Seeing our smiles and our arms around each other's shoulders, his Mama wiped her hands on her apron, his Dad went back to smoking his pipe and Julie Ann continued playing with her dolls. All was right on the farm.

Whistling through the field on my way home, I popped out of the corn on our side. I noticed my Mama was wiping her hands on her apron just as Mrs. Ryan had done. Seeing my smile, her face lit up and she went back through the screen door into the house. Little did I know she and Mrs. Ryan had already spent time on the phone solving our problems with a basket of eggs and a bushel of tomatoes. Yes, all was right on our farm as well.

Setting the tomatoes down on the back porch, I saw there already two more baskets from our own fields, and I knew Mama had been instrumental in patching up a long-time friendship. Mama came to the back door and gave me a thumb's up. All I could muster while hanging my head was, "What was I thinking? Sure wish that fight had never happened." Mama's soft voice said, "Just forgive and forget. It's tough to forgive ourselves, so it's probably best to start with other people. It's almost like peeling an onion. Layer by layer, forgiving others, you really do get to the point where you can forgive yourself."

So if you've argued with a friend or disagreed with a family member, and you've been offered an open hand today my readers, it probably means you have a good friend indeed. Forgive them, forgive yourself, peel back the layers of that onion and move on. I don't doubt there might be a basket of eggs or a bushel of tomatoes in your future. You just never know.

Life Lesson #37

America's Birthday

When I was a child, we couldn't afford many real fireworks. Oh, we got firecrackers and a few bottle rockets, but there was one year Daddy took his bonus and we drove down the main highway out of Smyrna, Tennessee, and located a for real honest fireworks store. When we all climbed out of the 1954 Chevy, I noticed Mama had on her best Sunday hat. I asked her about it and she just smiled and pushed me on into the store. We bought our fireworks, rockets, cherry bombs, sparkler fountains and one huge rocket with Chinese writing on the side.

We had a time that night and at the end when the big Chinese rocket went off, I looked up at my smiling Mama silhouetted against the sky and that Sunday hat just sparkled on her head. Mama had worn her best hat to honor America, that was the best she had and she was proud.

So on this 4th of July be proud. Wish America Happy Birthday with a Sunday hat, fireworks or a hug for loved ones. This Mama's boy stands proud today.

Life Lesson #38

Whisper

Being alone on a holiday is at best difficult and at worst, well, let's not howl at the Moon, so let's just say today was somewhere in the middle. Having the gift of gab I can talk to any and everyone. In fact, Mama used to say I could talk the ears off a Mule. Every once in a while a little loneliness creeps in. Now, I don't say this for pity but to make a point, we've all been there. It's how you end the day that matters.

While at the gym torturing my knees, I swear I heard a whisper in my ear. Then a few seconds later there it was again. Hmmm, I thought, either a breakdown is imminent or the elliptical needs a good dose of oil, like my knees. I heard it again in the shower and again in the car on the way to dinner. Then I remembered something my little Mama used to do, and it all made sense.

When I had a bad day as a child, Mama would hold me close and whisper in my ear, nothing at first, just a sound, and finally the word "hope". I would start laughing at the senseless whisper and by the time Mama breathed hope into my ears all my troubles were gone. Today, Mama whispered and hope answered.

Particularly trying day? Let me send a whispered hope your way. Works every time. Now, on to my burger and broccoli. I have to make a stab at being healthy, right?

Life Lesson #39

Locked in Your Heart

Several months before Mama passed and during a time when she was experiencing a lot of pain, she asked me to go into her bottom dresser drawer and bring her the big jewelry box. I was really excited since I knew she had been an avid collector of good jewelry for years, and I rarely got to inspect her pieces. This time she opened the bottom drawer of that ancient jewelry box and pulled out an old picture of the most handsome curly headed blonde young man I had ever seen.

Mama's eyes sparkled, a sad smile crossed her face, and she said, "Forever locked in my heart." She looked up at me from her wheelchair and told me the story of her first and heartfelt love. Billy "Curly" Sanderson. They were high school sweethearts but he had not returned from WWII.

She never told Daddy because he always thought he was her first love and she didn't want him to be jealous of someone long gone. First loves are special though and never forgotten. She said, "Son, he is forever locked in my heart, and that's the easiest place for something best left alone. Not forgotten but cherished. Not hidden but secret. Not denied but accepted. Not shared yet treasured beyond belief."

Mama knew I was missing the love of my life long dead these many years, as well, so she shared hers with me. I never once thought the love of her life wasn't my Dad, but there he was, a curly headed Adonis, and my mother obviously had kept him secret for the majority of her life.

Mama patted my hand and simply said, "Lock your heart but know the key is a heartbeat away." To know my Mama and I shared this type of inner battle and hers far longer than mine, helped me to move on from my loss, lock that love away and live again.

So tonight, lock your memories in your heart, cry if need be, but hold your head high and know that in the morning that sweet everlasting love will still be there, safe and strong. Good night, this man is tired and my memories full...

Life Lesson #40

Quit to Start

My singing voice is far from operatic and during a recital at the age of 9 seeing the reaction of the audience when I couldn't hit the right note with a brick bat, I told Mama I was going to quit. She gave me the "look" and simply said, "Baby, your greatest fear should not be fear of failure, but of succeeding at things in life that don't really matter. If you quit, you are on your way to starting and that's worth the time."

So having found a place to quit today, it's time to start something that really matters. Get about your day…this man sees a starting gate, not the finish line.

Life Lesson #41

Lonely or Not

After moving in with my Mama to aid in her care and after a particularly bad day at work, I came home, threw my briefcase in the corner (literally threw it). When I looked up, Mama's little eyes were lit up like fire. I told her I didn't need "the look" and that I never felt so lonely. She held out both arms, the Mama signal a hug was imminent, and said, "Little one, the difference in being alone and lonely is easy to discern. Alone is when you look around and not a soul is in sight but your thoughts are loud and clear. Lonely is when you look around and see people everywhere but hear nothing in your heart. That's when you have to pick up the song of life and sing it loud." She began humming quietly to herself and continued her crochet oblivious to any further questions.

So whether you're alone, lonely or can't carry a tune in a bucket, fill the space around you with sound. You might reach someone else's lonely ear. What a nice thought to start the day my friends.

Life Lesson #42

Happiness

Growing up I had an Uncle Dee. He was a simple man and took great joy in just about everything he did. I never met a happier person, whether sitting in the middle of town counting cars coming through or wandering the farm looking for stray baby rabbits to return to their nests (he always kept a pair of gloves in his pocket so the mama rabbit wouldn't reject any babies he happened to relocate). In fact, he loved life so much and never seemed sad or depressed that everybody in town used to make fun of him, calling him, Happy Dee, Smiling Dee, Old Fool, or Clown. You name it; some people are truly cruel by nature.

One Saturday our family went to town to do our weekly shopping, and there sat Uncle Dee at the train station, sporting that goofy smile, waiting for the local freight train so he could count the cars. He waived at everybody who drove by, but especially at Mama. She enthusiastically waived back as we passed. He was oblivious to the nods and winks as the passersby came and went. After we drove by, I laughed to my brother and pointed, "There's that old clown again." Out of nowhere, I felt it – my Mama slapped the back of my head so hard, had we known anything about whiplash at the time, I could have made a civil case no doubt. Mama squealed for Daddy to stop the car and yanked me out by one arm so hard I knew my arm had to be six inches longer than the other. Up came that index finger and Mama's words stung like a bee, "Young man, the primary cause of happiness or sadness isn't the situation but how you feel about it. If you don't understand that, you'll never be happy or sad. You'll just exist like all these other people passing by. And if your happiness depends on the sadness of others, I pity your life. Think on that young man and get your behind in that back seat."

I visited that same spot in the middle of town recently, and watching the cars driving by, I began to waive and smile at each one of them. I noticed some waived in return, others stared straight ahead, but with each little gesture of happiness, a simple wave, I could see Mama's wisdom. I may not be in the best situation, but if I change my mindset, I'll find joy in whatever I'm doing. So today's thoughts are happy ones, but just know as I hold my coffee mug this morning, I still think my right arm is longer because of that lesson.

Life Lesson #43

See Through My Eyes

Several years after my father passed away, my Mama started sitting in front of the mirror and studying her face. She would try on different outfits, color her hair (rarely), try new lipstick (often), but whatever she did, it had to be in front and center the big 1950's dresser mirror Daddy bought her years before. I watched it over and over and finally said, "Mama, why are you constantly looking at yourself." The reply I got both surprised me and made me understand just how deeply a person can love.

Mama sighed sitting in front of that mirror then said, "I'm trying to capture the me reflected in your father's eyes. No matter how many wrinkles on my face, I was young and beautiful to him our entire life together. I want to see the me he saw. From the day we met my reflection in your father's eyes was tinted with pure love."

Take a good look tonight through someone else's eyes. Like what you see?

Life Lesson #44

Rainbows and Rain

This weekend Mother Nature rained out several key things I had wanted to do with my best friend. I was so disappointed and frustrated I couldn't enjoy anything else for worrying about that. Standing on the porch with this friend, who was just as disappointed as I was and who rarely showed his true emotions, I heard him say, "Well, it's nothing but a thing."

His ability to accept the negative and look for a positive reminded me of my Mama. She used to say, "Baby, you can't have a rainbow without first going through rain!" The light in her eyes when she spoke that truth was the same light in my friend's eyes.

So when you're experiencing a "rainy day event," look for the rainbow. It's nothing but a thing.

Life Lesson #45

New Day

The day before my Mama passed away she gave me one of her most profound life lessons. I could tell Mama was very uncomfortable, and I kept asking her what I could do to make things better. As is normal with me, I tried too hard and finally she just smiled one of those "Mama" smiles and said, "My baby, when Mama is gone, always remember this, don't start your day with the broken pieces of yesterday. Every day is a fresh start. Each day is a new beginning. Every morning we wake up is the first day of a new life. Leave the broken pieces of yesterday in the past." I love you Mama, and I miss you on this and every day since.

Open your eyes today, friends, to the possibilities and sweep up any broken pieces. Time for my walk and fresh coffee...

Life Lesson #46

Fly

One summer day after all the farm chores were done, Daddy and my brother took our old rickety truck to help gather hay with a neighbor. I was too young at the time so I got to spend the day with my Mama. Having gotten into as much trouble as a 5-year old can get into at the barn, I was bored and started begging Mama for ideas. Mama grabbed up the picnic basket she had already filled to my surprise and off to the pond we went for a hot July day picnic lunch.

We hadn't been there long when I fell in the pond, came up covered in mud crying, only to find my Mama laughing and crying at my dilemma. That made it worse, and I really started having a baby fit. Mama laughed even louder so I cried even louder. This went on a while till I gave up, calmed down and got quiet. Once I did that, Mama smiled, cleaned me up by dunking me BACK into the pond and said, "Baby, you're crying because you think you did something wrong and you didn't know how to fix it, you didn't see any options to solve the problem. Honey, look at that bumble bee. He's so fat with those little wings there's no way he should be able to fly. But he doesn't know that. He believes he can fly, so he does." She smiled, kissed my wet head and off to the house we went for fresh clothes and an afternoon nap, the sound of that fat bumble bee in the background.

So, believe you can fly today, take off and enjoy every amazing minute. I'm flying no matter what may come my way. I hope you are too.

Life Lesson #47

Eyes in the Mirror

This old man had a rough night as I'm sure the reader must from time to time. In the middle of the night I was faced with an epiphany, that I am not always proud of the person I am, sometimes not even recognizing myself, but I can only try to improve one day at a time.

My Mama used to say that often when the mirror reflects an image you don't like, you can always buy a new mirror, but it's the eyes in the mirror that need changing. I plan to make some changes starting today.

Have a cup of coffee for me this morning and see what your eyes reflect. I'm trying to see beyond…

Life Lesson #48

Good Friends and Good Memories for Life's End

Visiting my friends and family in and near Smyrna, Tennessee this weekend, I stopped at a crossroads near the top of a hill on Old Nashville Highway and Enon Springs Road. The area hardly recognizable now from my childhood memories. As I looked around this little intersection, once the thriving community of Hilltop, I was transported back to how it once was, a stone and rock gas station on one corner with a family home/television repair shop on the opposite corner. But my best memory was of the store at the top of the hill, Taliaferro's, or lovingly called by most as simply Hilltop Market.

Historically, during the time right before integration when segregation was prevalent all over the South, this was an area mainly of color. But the Hilltop Market owned by Pete and Blanche Taliaferro was neither all white nor all black, but a melting pot of cultures, frequented by every race, poor or rich. The Taliaferro's were loved by everyone in that community. Always kind to everyone, they would even let the poorer families run groceries on credit, on a tab if you will. My family was one of these. We were by no means affluent, but as a six-year old I never knew just how hard things were, and Mama and Daddy always did their best to keep that part of life a secret. In fact, even though we ran a tab, very large sometimes, Daddy was always able to pay off our credit with his Christmas bonus from his day job at Lane Cedar Company in Smyrna, another town landmark long gone.

At Christmas, once Daddy had paid our tab with his bonus, Mama would buy all the fixings for our Christmas feast and unbeknownst to this young boy, she would help Santa shop for his Christmas gifts to the children right there at Hilltop Market. So no matter what I saw in the Sears Wishbook every year, what I got looked surprisingly familiar as some little treasure that used to reside on the Market's shelves.

Christmas of 1961, I was six years old. That year, above the main counter at the Market, I found a bright red remote controlled battery driven Lincoln Continental with suicide doors. It was huge, almost two and a half feet long and even had a plastic man in the driver' seat and working headlights. I wanted that car with every bit of my six-year old's heart, but when I told Mama and Daddy, I noticed them steal looks at each other. With a price tag of almost $20, it was far too expensive and just wasn't destined to fit in Santa's bag for me.

Each grocery visit that cold December I would pull Mama over to where it was and beg. She'd pat my head and give me a sad smile. She'd say, "Honey, that's an expensive toy, and I don't think Santa could even get it down our chimney, but don't worry, Santa won't forget you." I did notice she'd wipe back a tear or two, but it was really the way her voice got caught in her throat that let me know the red Lincoln might not make it under our tree. It was probably going home with one of the rich kids who made fun of me anyway. That in itself made me mad but as with a typical six-year old, the taunts never lasted long in my little head, and I would be on to the next event anyway.

Now, Mr. Pete and Miss Blanche, collectively the Taliaferro's, and the owners of the Market, were our good friends. Every time we'd go for groceries even though we bought on credit, they treated us like family and never mentioned our growing debt. In fact, most times we went, Miss Blanche would pick me up right away and sit me on her checkout counter while Mama shopped. Miss Blanche would talk to me but mostly listen and let me share all the hopes and dreams of a six-year old boy. That month I told her how much I wanted that Lincoln. I noticed her glance at my Mama as I touted the wonders of battery driven remote control. My Mama would just smile, lower her eyes at Miss Blanche, shake her head and sigh. Our tab that year was over $500 and Daddy's bonus would barely cover that. I had no idea that even Christmas dinner that year was going to be slight, let alone presents.

Come Christmas morning though with fires in the fireplaces and gas stoves lit all around, I jumped out of bed warm and toasty. Running to the tree I found oranges and tangerines, chocolate candy and even candied orange slices. Santa had left me a cowboy hat, holster and a 45 cap pistol. All great presents, but no red Lincoln. I guess the disappointment on my face was evident because Mama grabbed a handkerchief out of her apron and began wiping her eyes. Daddy took her hand and held her close. I also noticed there was nothing under the tree for either Mama or Daddy, something they didn't seem concerned about at all though. As Christmas Day unfolded, the smells of Christmas dinner made me forget about the red Lincoln, and I put those orange candy slices to good use indeed. My brother and I also played "Old West" with my hat and pistol till we were both exhausted.

All of a sudden I noticed a truck was slowly making its way up our snow covered driveway. I heard Daddy laugh as he opened the door and say, "Now, Pete, I paid my bill, didn't I?" The couple standing at the door both laughed. Christmas visitors indeed! It was Mr. Pete and Miss Blanche Taliaferro. She had a big coconut cake and handed it to my Mama. That was my Mama's favorite. Mr. Pete pulled out from behind his back a brand new small tool box with a bow on it, perfect to fit on Daddy's barn work bench. There was a lot of hugging and tears all around. I shot both of them with my cap pistol and started to run off so the grownups could visit when Miss Blanche stopped me. She grabbed me and hugged me so tight I knew I had surely done something wrong. I also noticed the puzzled looks on the faces of both Mama and Daddy.

After letting go, she pulled me to the door and said, "My boy, Santa made a second stop this morning at our store and asked me to bring you something. He said he couldn't get it down your chimney no matter how hard he pushed. On that snow covered porch sat that shiny red remote controlled Lincoln with the suicide doors! My mouth dropped open. So did my Daddy's. Mama had to sit down she was so surprised. Miss Blanche just laughed and said, "Boy, you better get it inside, there's more snow coming." I yelled, and in no time that Lincoln was whizzing around our Christmas tree. Mama and Miss Blanche went crying and hugging to the kitchen and Daddy and

Mr. Pete shook hands for a good ten minutes. Little did they know though I could hear Santa in my head telling me he hadn't forgot me. The miracle of a Smyrna Christmas for that young boy is now a good memory of good friends for this old man that will live in my heart until life's end.

Always look around your changing landscape. Times change and so does the scenery for every town, but as my Mama was fond of saying, the memories remain forever the same, richer with time. Much richer.

Life Lesson #49

Rise Up and Dance

Today, Aretha passed away. Miss Franklin. The Queen of Soul. Few celebrity deaths affect me anymore. I'm hardened I thought at my age to death when it's someone I don't personally know, someone I never met, someone who had no clue I was here either and whose life I never affected. But… Aretha was different. Her life, her voice, her talent, even her soul affected mine immensely. She could bring me to tears with song and then again make my soul dance with unbridled joy. In fact, I can well remember a moment she may have even saved my sanity.

In November 1994 I lost the love of my life to a slow and painful death. Passing away was a release, but for me, I thought surely my own life would cease in conjunction. That cold November morning after the funeral as I tried to decide how I would keep going, my Mama knocked on my door bright and early. She had driven herself to my house, no small feat, Mama hadn't really driven into downtown Nashville much by herself, but she knew I was hurting and she was on a mission. When I opened my door she immediately backed me up into my tiny living room. Mama was carrying a cassette tape in her right hand, her little old lady purse dangling from her elbow. She simply said, "I'll take a cup of coffee, and I'll put this on to play."

As I sat Mama's coffee mug on the sofa table and turned around, true to her word Mama had put the cassette tape in. She had carefully queued the tape to start at the song's beginning and out poured Aretha's voice. "Baby baby sweet baby…Since you've been gone."

Mama started snapping her fingers to the music, nodding her head. She raised her left hand in affirmation like she was in church and closed her eyes. She started moving, her left hand held high and started humming along to the song. I stood there, broken hearted, thinking my soul hurts so bad, it's beyond repair. Yet Mama was dancing and humming and snapping those fingers. I was just about to tell Mama how I felt when she started singing along with Miss Franklin. Mama had a sweet voice but this time her voice had true soul in it. Quietly at first, but then louder and more real she sang along,

"Baby baby, sweet baby
There's something that I just got to say
Baby baby, sweet baby
You left me hurtin' in a real cold way."

I stopped with my mouth open and no words forthcoming. Aretha's voice, Mama's voice, the words and the music started filling that empty hole in my heart, in my soul. Emotion started building in me, coming up and out as tears, as sadness, as grief and yes as love.

Mama opened her eyes, grabbed my hand, her little purse still dangling from her elbow, she turned me round and round. She was singing and crying. I was singing and crying. Both of us dancing and snapping our fingers in time to the music. I knew at that moment the love of my life was in Heaven smiling, fingers snapping to the same music, still loving me, no matter the time, no matter the distance, even beyond life, beyond death.

This was what Aretha could do, her voice could transport you beyond pain, beyond joy, just beyond. My Mama knew how I was hurting, and she was there for me. So was Aretha that day. That memory surfaced today when I heard the news the Queen of Soul had passed. I can hear Mama's fingers snapping and her little voice singing along to Miss Franklin,

"Speak your name
And I'll feel a thrill
You said I do
And I said I will
I tell you that I'll stay true
And give you just a little time
Wait on me baby
I want you to be all of mine

Baby baby, sweet baby"

Goodbye Aretha, say hello to my Mama, you two have a few things in common.

Let your heart sing today. Tell everyone you love how special they truly are. Put an Aretha song on your lips and dance. The Queen of Soul truly lives on.

Life Lesson #50

❦

Dance Inside Your Heart

L istening to the rain on the metal roof of my little porch and watching the vines of my morning glories sway in the breeze, purple and crimson flowers waving at me as they dance in the early pre-dawn light, I noticed outlined against the sky above my neighbor's roof a tiny heart-shaped leaf. A stray vine pulled itself away from its family, otherwise wrapped tightly around the porch post. That single heart-shape leaf transported me back in memory to my third grade class, specifically to a winter PTA (Parent Teachers Association) meeting when my then-teacher, Miss Thelma Davis, was relating her students' class progress to the visiting parents, some interested of course, others fidgeting to get home, their intent on something other than student reports.

My Mama attended every PTA meeting and served as a chaperone on every student outing. She somehow managed to not only take care of her children's daily life from home, but she never missed a chance to monitor and improve our school work as well. I could hear Mama and Miss Thelma discussing my test scores in Math (not so good), geography (shows genuine interest), history (outstanding and inquisitive, that sounded good), spelling (average, no spell check or autocorrect in those days), and art (progressive but repetitive). From the look on my Mama's face that had to be bad. Mama's troubled gaze made me wonder if a whipping was coming once we left, so I started really paying attention instead of punching my friend Frank in the arm, something he returned repeatedly, laughing and grinning as only nine-year old boys can do.

Mama pulled Miss Thelma away from the few remaining parents, picked up three pieces of my artwork and began to question the teacher's description. Mama said, "Miss Davis, you say my son's artwork is progressive. I completely agree even though your tone seems derogatory in nature. Progressive means enlightening to me and indeed his use of color and form brings to mind a Sunset on a Spring day when the sun's light and the coming of night create a heart-felt ambience to which you can surely relate. Now, I heard all these words and looked at the red, yellow and blue swirling inside a heart I had drawn. Trying to picture what my Mama had said, I realized I had no clue at all what that meant, nor what she saw, but it surely was good from the pride I could see in Mama's face. It appeared Miss Thelma's open mouth suggested she was planning a retort. Mama stopped her with one upturned finger and continued, "And this drawing would show far more than common aptitude with its lines and heart-felt rendering." Wow, I had no idea what "heart-felt rendering" could be. My gaze went to the drawing I had done of a purple and green heart with a very crooked arrow through the middle. I remembered my crayon broke in mid arrow and I had to finish it with the nubs.

Hearts, I noticed all of my drawings were nothing more than hearts with color in them, around them or splashed over them. Not army men, cars, guns or lions and tigers as many of my classmates had drawn. Just hearts. I made a mental note to draw something else in our next art class when I heard Miss Thelma finally interject the following, "Mrs. Toombs I know you must see more in these than I, but I'm tasked with trying to broaden your son's limited talent." With that my Mama's eyes flashed, her finger went up, shaking just a bit this time, and I heard all my Mama's love pour forth like Niagara Falls. "Miss Davis, limited talent is when you squelch artistic expression of any kind as you obviously do in your classes. It appears from all the other artwork, your students see only the common place things, guns, cars, animals and houses, albeit a few do show promise with spaceships and aliens. My son's heart drawings show an array of emotions, not the least of which is love. Why look what he's done here. He's mixed color inside this heart giving the viewer a peaceful and calm feeling. In this one the arrow is crooked indicative of life's journeys and toils." (So that's what a broken crayon can do I thought). "These just make me happy when I see them."

Miss Thelma grabbed that moment and in an exasperated voice said, "But Mrs. Toombs they're ALL hearts." Her eyes wide open now, it appeared she felt she had made her point when Mama gave this final comment right before she lovingly folded and placed each one of my heart drawings in her purse. "Yes, exactly, Miss Davis, these drawings show just how creativity and art dance inside my son's heart, no matter what he sees."

With that Miss Thelma looked from my Mama to me and said, "I never thought about it like that." Mama said, "It's not the outer appearance of a person that defines who they are or will be, but what's inside their heart that counts." And off we went home, ending the day with a big bowl of ice cream at the kitchen table as Mama lovingly taped each of my heart drawings to our refrigerator. Mama looked at me as I pushed my empty bowl away and rubbed my tummy. "Son, I love you for who you are, for what you feel and for what's inside your heart, no matter what, no matter when, no matter where. Always let your heart dance." Mama hugged me so tight that all I could muster was, "I love you too, Mama."

So as you read this, I hope you'll dance inside your own heart and always let others see your true vision. No telling what the world will see if you do.

Life Lesson #51

Church in a Purse

I'm sure everyone has rough moments in their lives, moments that seem so dark no light whatsoever is going to shine through with hope. Suicides are at an all time high, mass shootings, robberies, senseless murders, assaults and abuse. It's enough to make one want to stay in bed, covered head to foot. We wouldn't be human if we didn't have dark moments I suppose, but knowing that, we've got to believe a better day is coming, the sun will be bright again, hope will find us in the darkness, and we will keep going. We've got to believe this and it's our duty as human beings to get up, keep moving and to help those around us to get up as well, to give hope and spread the word that change is coming, the morning will show itself and little by little, step by step we'll move on, alone or together hand in hand, whether by pulling, pushing, cajoling or inspiring. We can get through any adversity, yes even alone. Ah, but there's what this life lesson is all about. Alone or together, choice will get us through. Now, that little speech sounds good and perhaps there's a life lesson in that too, but that's just a side bar…

Sitting in my recliner I can see from one side of my house to the other, even front to back. Yes, my tiny house is so small you could hear an ant crawling in the living room even if you were headed out the back door to the porch. Residing on the wall in the front room is an old banjo clock that belonged to my grandmother. It not only chimes me awake every morning at 6:00 am (thankfully, the maker supplied a clever little device that shuts off the chimes from 10 pm until 6 am) but if you're having a restless night anyway, the ticking is worse than the pitter patter of that ant I mentioned earlier.

Not being able to sleep last night with much tossing and turning due to the base of a car stereo somewhere in the neighborhood at 2 in the morning, I was wide awake. I could actually feel the base of that stereo. Boom, boom, boom. Trust me, if I could have gotten my hands on that stereo or its owner, this life lesson would never have been written since I'm sure neither pens nor notebooks are allowed in city jail. But as the booming base began to quiet, it took back seat to the ticking of that old banjo clock. Steady, rhythmic and persistent. Tick. Tick. Tick. Nary one Tock. Always tick, tick, tick. Unrelenting. My mind began to wander and with every tick of that old clock, memories began appearing in my head, the day's events, happenings from my childhood, moments with friends, snippets of conversations, all starting as still photographs, some old, some new. Each of them changing with every tick of that clock. A scenario began to shape itself bit by bit, like an animator's sketchbook, the type of book where each page has characters in various poses so the faster you turn the pages the figures move and run and dance. Lifelike movement indeed. I was headed back to a specific moment in time. That moment was the day after my father had taken his own life, a truly horrific day for me. I was asking Mama about God and church. I was angry at both and railing against belief in any Spirit that would allow something like this to happen. I was mad at the world and when my Mama had lovingly tried to console me, even though her own soul was broken as well, she had tried to guide me into talking to her God for help. That set me off on a tirade of denial. The more I talked, the more desperate I became. Through all this sat my Mama, tears in her eyes, staunch and stoic, her hands resting on a little purse on her lap, a purse she never went anywhere without.

Mama and I both knew I wasn't angry with her, she was my only and last hope for sanity at that moment, but she, as well as I, knew all that bitterness and bile in my heart had to come up and out for healing to begin after such an event. All during my ranting, there she sat, never moving, not leaving my side. Holding onto that little purse, she waited for the moment, that single fleeting moment only a Mama knows and believes will come, to save her child. True to her belief, that moment arrived.

Pacing around the room, my rage reaching an almost hysterical crescendo, I looked at my Mama and on her lap that little purse, the same purse she had carried for years. Mama had many purses, but this one had become her favorite. Daddy had given it to her on a Christmas long before. She took it everywhere with her but especially now. A small dark leather bag with two sturdy handles. I laughingly called it "an old lady bag". Every Southern lady had one, not a shoulder bag, not a clutch, just a plain bag with two strong handles. The type of bag a Mama could use to direct a wayward child down the aisle at church with a quick thump to your head and still be fashionable in doing so. Yes, I remembered that bag and was thumped with it on more than one occasion. So, I pointed at it and I pronounced what I thought would end this tirade. I said, "Mama, you believe in your God so strongly and in your church, if you can pull either God or church out of that handbag for me, something tangible I can see, touch, smell or feel, then and only then will I believe ever again!"

Silence.

One tear ran down Mama's face and she cleared her throat. She patted the sofa cushion next to her for me to sit, and she began talking. In reality, she began saving my soul. I was shaking when I sat next to her. Mama grabbed my hand and held on tight for a moment; then she opened that purse and peered into its depths with those tiny blue eyes. I thought in my anger she was stalling. She couldn't possibly answer my demand. The child in me, though, was praying she could answer, and that child was not disappointed.

Mama reached into that purse and started pulling items from the darkness one by one, and as if speaking to herself, she glanced occasionally at me to make sure I was listening. The first thing out was her wallet. Mama looked at it as if she had never seen it before and said, "No, God is not found in money. Even the Good Book tells me that. Why, God even chased the money men from the Temple, so no He's not in there. But seeing that does remind me that I'm blessed to have a few dollars and all my bills are current so whatever is left over in there I should give to someone less fortunate than I. But no, God's definitely not in that, but maybe in the reminder…"

Out came a pillbox, one I had given her when I was a young child. "Well, hmmm," she said as she opened that tiny porcelain pillbox, "No,

I don't think church is hiding in there though the memory of your sweet face when you spent a month's allowance on it as a birthday gift for me is heartwarming. Do you remember? You had worked one whole month with your Daddy digging potatoes at eight years old. That pleases my heart, and I can see your Daddy laughing as you presented it to me after church service that day. Every time I open it for an ache or pain I think of that."

Next was an embroidered handkerchief she lovingly pulled from inside. "Well, now we're getting there," she said. "This is the last of a dozen handkerchiefs Mama Toombs gave to me when I married your Daddy. She had by her own hand embroidered 'Married with God's Love' on each one. Yes, indeed, over the years I've dabbed your tears, my tears and the tears of others, especially when Mama Toombs passed into glory. I've washed your face with them, washed it free from sorrow and pain many times. And I've held each handkerchief to my breast during happy times and sad ones. I've used it to wave goodbye when my family left me one by one and waved it again when they returned, if they were able. Even as I'll use it to wave farewell to your Daddy, until we meet once again. Yes, this is the very last one, all the others have been stored away, too frayed with wear to keep using. Over 40 years they've lasted, but is that God or church? Maybe, maybe not, but the love in each one surely is a part of that Spirit.

And on and on through that purse she would pull out things and quietly tell a story about each one, never saying any one of them WAS God or church, but explaining how the feelings evoked by each one was a piece in that puzzle. And so she preached, using what she had, her little purse and the goodness within. She preached for God to heal my heart and to fill the emptiness I had. The emotion within her words and the love in her eyes melted that icy grip of madness on my soul, and I started weeping, my heart broken at the loss of my daddy. The grieving had finally begun. My Mama's words had allowed me to travel with her through the years and her sweet memories of her children and her husband. Mama was determined to reunite me with Spirit. She did just that with her little purse. God was truly in there as he was in everything, trees, animals, every little thing.

The moment began to fade as an old photograph will and the

animator's sketchbook pages slowed to a standstill. And then… Tick, Tick, Tick. The old banjo clock on the wall in my tiny house. In the distance that base of a car stereo. I was back, but the lesson was learned. God is in each of us, some a little more, some a little less perhaps, but that spirit is there.

I jumped up and ran to the back bedroom where I opened an old wardrobe that had belonged to my Mama. There in the very back was that sweet old lady handbag and I smiled. "Mama," I said, "only you could preach Church in a Purse." I shut the door of that old wardrobe, now content. I no longer needed to search anywhere for Spirit. I had found it. As I started my coffee, the sun was peeking in my kitchen window. I looked out at its glory and thought, "Yes, Mama, I hear you."

Life Lesson #52

Never Too Big For My Heart

A close friend recently sent me the sweetest picture of her grandson learning how to blow bubbles with bubblegum. She said he was quite proud of himself, and even though the bubble hid any possibility of seeing his smile, the look in his eyes indicated he was not only proud but he now had a skill learned for life. Not much of a skill you say? Read on then and you might see just how important the little things in life can be.

Not the brightest lamp in the house was surely a statement the other kids taunted me with as I was growing up. By far not the cruelest bullying remark I ever got. Those would come much later as some children grew into hate and prejudice learned from parents, but luckily I got past all of that, somewhat no worse for wear. Once I was home back then though, the bullying went away, so I can only imagine how hard it must be for those bullied today. With social media (I use the term "social" with a tinge of sad irony) the bullying can be constant and cruel.

I will admit I did take longer than most to learn basic skills like riding a bike, milking a cow or even planting seeds in a row, this last shortcoming due to the fact I would get sidetracked, and I liked to hide seeds where I thought birds could find them easily for food. However, even though I was slow to learn basic skills, learn them I did. My parents took much time and effort to make sure I learned, no matter what they had to do and no matter how long it took. They were concerned and caring. As for the bike riding issues, well, we were fairly poor, and even though we couldn't afford a brand new bike, my Daddy came across one at an abandoned house not too far from our farm. He brought it home, cleaned it up, painted it baby blue, my favorite color at the time, and hand fashioned training wheels to help me. Everything he did to make it easier for me to learn, and with his help and Mama's sideline encouragement, it wasn't long before the training wheels were a thing of the past and I was proudly riding the "Blue Bomber" everywhere. Even though some only saw a used bicycle, I had hours of excitement and fun thanks to patience and perseverance.

When I started first grade at six years old, I was faced with new challenges, each one harder than the one before it in my eyes, but each one guided and aided by my Mama and Daddy. A challenge I definitely remember from that time was bubblegum. I desperately wanted to be one of the "cool kids" and blow bubbles so I could make them pop. Perhaps being cool meant annoying the teachers as well, but I just wanted to fit in somewhere.

At that time bubblegum was quite a treat and even though it was readily available at the grocery, we rarely had a spare penny for a handful of gum When we did though, my Mama would sneak a penny into my pocket and it was my choice what kind of gum to get. I cared little for the trading cards that accompanied some brands of gum. I just wanted as much as I could stuff in my mouth so I could prepare for my sessions in bubble blowing and popping. I was amazed at the size of bubbles my brother could muster, but as I always thought he was full of hot air anyway, I shouldn't have been surprised (sorry, bubba, but you know it's true).

After chewing and chewing and chewing I just couldn't manage even one bubble, not one. I was a failure and the kids at school would surely seize upon this for more teasing. I gave up and went to the barn to sulk. That's where Mama found me sniffling and sad. Plopping down beside me on the hay, Mama wanted to know why bubblegum was important enough that I would cry about it. "I JUST CAN'T DO IT," I said, "I can't even blow a bubble, and the kids are all going to make fun of me for it like they do for everything else." Mama wiped my tears with her apron and in true Mama words said, "Can't never did do nothing, so quit pouting. Do you have any more gum?" I told her I did and handed her half of what I had left. She popped a piece in her mouth and chewed, then chewed some more and next thing I knew she had the biggest bubble ever. When it popped with a loud "smack" it covered her face. For a minute I thought she'd be mad but then she laughed; I laughed too. So there sat my Mama in the hay not only teaching me how to get bubbles out of bubblegum but teaching me not to ever give up on something I wanted. She worked with me, and after a while I started making the best pink bubbles you could imagine. They got bigger and bigger and with each pop we laughed until our sides ached. Mama pulled me onto her lap and we laughed and talked all afternoon. She told me to always keep trying, never give up, that everything was possible to those who tried. I've lived by that for well over 60 years now.

The most important lesson I learned that day though, far from the pink bubblegum or even try try again, was when Mama told me, while holding me close, "One day soon you'll be too big for Mama's lap, but you'll never be too big for Mama's heart."

So whether it's blowing bubbles, riding a bike, getting a job, or saving for the future, keep trying. Help those around you as they try as well, whatever the task at hand. You may be the very one who can keep someone else moving forward in life. Remember, no matter who that person is or what their situation may be, just like a small boy learned long ago on his Mama's lap, they're never too big for your heart.

CPSIA information can be obtained
at www.ICGtesting.com
Printed in the USA
LVHW031513300321
682969LV00002B/544